LAUGH
–OUT–
LOUD
PUNS,
JOKES,
and
RIDDLES
for
KIDS

Books by Rob Elliott

LAUGH —OUT— LOUD PUNS, JOKES, *and* RIDDLES *for* KIDS

ROB ELLIOTT

Revell

a division of Baker Publishing Group
Grand Rapids, Michigan

© 2023 by Robert E. Teigen

Published by Revell
a division of Baker Publishing Group
PO Box 6287, Grand Rapids, MI 49516-6287
www.revellbooks.com

Printed in the United States of America

Library of Congress Cataloging-in-Publication Data
Names: Elliott, Rob (Humorist), author.
Title: Laugh-out-loud puns, jokes, and riddles for kids / Rob Elliott.
Description: Grand Rapids, MI : Revell, a division of Baker Publishing
    Group, [2023] | Audience: Ages: 9–12 | Audience: Grades: 4–6
Identifiers: LCCN 2022020831 | ISBN 9780800742546 (trade
    paperback) | ISBN 9781493439850 (ebook)
Subjects: LCSH: Wit and humor, Juvenile.
Classification: LCC PN6166 .E45535 2023 | DDC 818/.602—dc23/
    eng/20220801
LC record available at https://lccn.loc.gov/2022020831

Baker Publishing Group publications use paper produced from sustainable
forestry practices and post-consumer waste whenever possible.

23   24   25   26   27   28   29   7   6   5   4   3   2   1

Q: **What did the ocean say to the fishing boat?**

A: Nothing—it just waved.

Q: **What do you call a ladybug that won't clean up its room?**

A: A litterbug.

Knock knock.
  Who's there?
Uno.
  Uno who?
Uno who this is?

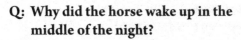

Q: **Why did the horse wake up in the middle of the night?**

A: It was having a night-mare.

Q: Where do dogs go if they lose their tails?

A: The re-tail store.

Q: What is the best thing to do with a blue whale?

A: Tell it a joke and cheer it up!

Q: What is a mouse's favorite game?

A: Hide and squeak.

Knock knock.
 Who's there?
Wayne.
 Wayne who?
Wayne drops are falling on my head, can you let me in?

Knock knock.
Who's there?
Whale.
Whale who?
Whale you let me tell you another knock-knock joke?

Knock knock.
Who's there?
Oliver.
Oliver who?
Oliver doors are locked, let me in!

Q: How much did Santa pay for his reindeer?

A: Just a few bucks. They didn't cost him much doe.

Q: How much did Santa's sleigh cost?

A: Nothing—it was on the house!

Q: Why did the skeleton refuse to go to the dance?

A: He had no-body to dance with.

Q: How do you know if you have an elephant in your refrigerator?

A: The refrigerator door won't shut!

Q: Why do silent frogs live forever?

A: Because they never croak!

Q: What's worse than raining cats and dogs?

A: Hailing taxi cabs.

Q: What does a racehorse like to eat for lunch?

A: Fast food.

Q: What do you call a greasy bug?

A: A butter-fly.

Knock knock.
  Who's there?
Gus.
  Gus who?
I bet you can't Gus who this is!

Knock knock.
  Who's there?
Della.
  Della who?
Open the door so I can Della
  'nother knock-knock joke.

Knock knock.
  Who's there?
Dots.
  Dots who?
Dots for me to know and you to find out.

Q: What is the difference between a fly and an eagle?

A: An eagle can fly, but a fly can't eagle.

Q: When can't you trust a farmer?

A: When he spills the beans!

Q: Why did the firefly get bad grades on his report card?

A: Because he wasn't very bright!

Q: What do you get when you cross a deer and a pirate?

A: A buck-aneer.

Joe: There were ten cats on a boat and one jumped off. How many were left?

Jack: I don't know, Joe. I guess nine?

Joe: No, there were none! They were all a bunch of copycats.

Q: Why were the chickens so tired?

A: They were working around the cluck.

Q: Why wouldn't the turkey eat any pumpkin pie?

A: It was too stuffed.

Q: Why did the elephants take up the least amount of room on Noah's ark?

A: Because they kept everything in their trunks!

Q: What did the bee say to the flower?
A: "Hi, honey!"

Q: What did the flower say to the bee?
A: "Buzz off!"

Knock knock.
　Who's there?
Scott.
　Scott who?
**There's Scott to be a better knock-
　knock joke than this one!**

Knock knock.
　Who's there?
Figs.
　Figs who?
Figs your doorbell, it's not working!

Knock knock.
Who's there?
Mabel.
Mabel who?
Mabel isn't working right either.

Knock knock.
Who's there?
Kenya.
Kenya who?
Kenya open the door, please?

Q: What do you get when you cross a pig with a Christmas tree?

A: A pork-u-pine.

Q: What is a maple's favorite class at school?

A: Geometree.

Q: What do little cows give?

A: Condensed milk.

Q: What did one nightcrawler say to the other nightcrawler?

A: "I know this great place down the road where we can eat dirt cheap!"

Knock knock.
  Who's there?
Owl.
  Owl who?
Owl tell you another joke if you let me in.

Knock knock.
  Who's there?
Reggie.
  Reggie who?
Reggie to open the door yet?

Knock knock.
  Who's there?
Randy.
  Randy who?
I Randy whole way here, so open up!

Q: **What do you get when your dog makes your breakfast?**

A: You get pooched eggs.

Q: **How do turkeys travel across the ocean?**

A: In a gravy boat.

Jill: **How do elephants smell?**

Jane: Not very good!

Q: **Why did Frosty go live in the middle of the ocean?**

A: Because snow man is an island!

Q: **What is a soda's favorite subject in school?**

A: Fizzics.

Q: **What do you get when you throw a couch in the pond?**

A: A sitting duck!

Q: **What do you get when you pour boiling water down a rabbit hole?**

A: Hot Cross Bunnies.

Q: What do you get when you step on a piano?

A: Foot-notes!

Knock knock.
  Who's there?
Police.
  Police who?
Police come out and play with me!

Knock knock.
  Who's there?
Darren.
  Darren who?
I'm Darren you to tell a funnier knock-knock joke!

Knock knock.
  Who's there?
Rita.
  Rita who?
Rita good book lately?

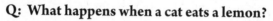

Q: What happens when a cat eats a lemon?
A: You get a sour-puss.

Q: How do dolphins make hard decisions?
A: By flippering a coin.

Q: What do you get when you throw a pig into the bushes?
A: A hedgehog.

Q: **How did the barber win the race?**

A: He took a short-cut.

Q: **What is a sailor's favorite kind of book to read?**

A: Ferry tales.

Q: **How do you sneak across the desert without being seen?**

A: You wear camel-flage.

Q: **What do you get when you spill your coffee in the dirt?**

A: Coffee grounds!

Tim: Did you hear about the guy who stuck his finger in a light socket?

Scott: No, what happened?

Tim: It was shocking!

Knock knock.
Who's there?
Bean.
Bean who?
It's bean way too long since you've heard a knock-knock joke!

Knock knock.
Who's there?
Bug spray.
Bug spray who?
Bug spray they won't get squished!

Q: What kind of keys never unlock anything?

A: Monkeys, turkeys, and donkeys.

Q: What happened to the dog after it swallowed the watch?

A: It was full of ticks.

Q: What kind of vegetable has the worst manners?

A: A rude-abaga.

Q: How does a cow get to the office?

A: On a cow-moo-ter train.

Knock knock.
  Who's there?
Turnip.
  Turnip who?
Turnip the heat—it's cold in here!

Knock knock.
  Who's there?
Sharon.
  Sharon who?
I'm Sharon my cookies if you'll let me in!

Knock knock.
  Who's there?
Juno.
  Juno who?
Juno who this is, so open up already!

Q: What did the spider say to the fly?
A: "Why don't you stick around for a while?"

Q: **What do you get when you cross a bear with a forest?**

A: You get fur trees.

Q: **What did the horse say when he tripped and fell down?**

A: "Help! I've fallen and I can't giddy-up!"

Q: **Why did the boy eat his homework?**

A: The teacher said it would be a piece of cake.

Q: **What happened when the turkey got in a fight?**

A: He got the stuffing knocked out of him.

Mark: What's the best place to chop down a Christmas tree?

Tim: I'm not sure.

Mark: About three inches off the ground.

Q: What kind of animal do you take into battle?

A: An army-dillo.

Q: What is big, gray, and wears glass slippers?

A: Cinderelephant.

Knock knock.
  Who's there?
Cargo.
  Cargo who?
Cargo beep, beep and vroom, vroom!

Knock knock.
Who's there?
Woo.
Woo who?
**Don't get all excited. It's just
a knock-knock joke!**

Knock knock.
Who's there?
Anna.
Anna who?
Anna one, Anna two, Anna three!

**Q: What animals do you find in a
monastery?**

A: Chip-monks!

**Q: Why didn't the crab spend any of his
money?**

A: Because he was a penny pincher.

Q: What kind of bird do you have with every meal?

A: A swallow.

Q: Why don't fish ever get a summer vacation?

A: They spend every day in schools.

Knock knock.
  Who's there?
Adore.
  Adore who?
Adore is between you and me so please open up!

Knock knock.
  Who's there?
Pumpkin.
  Pumpkin who?
A pumpkin fill up your flat tire.

Knock knock.
  Who's there?
Rich.
  Rich who?
Rich knock-knock joke is your favorite?

Q: Why did the boy stop using his pencil?

A: It was pointless.

Q: What happens when you cross a river and a stream?

A: You get wet feet!

Q: What did the rattlesnakes do after they had a fight?

A: They hissed and made up.

Q: What kind of trees wear mittens?
A: Palm trees.

Knock knock.
   Who's there?
Watson.
   Watson who?
Watson TV tonight?

Knock knock.
   Who's there?
Olive.
   Olive who?
Since Olive here, I think you should let me in!

Knock knock.
   Who's there?
Justin.
   Justin who?
I think I got here Justin time!

Q: **What do you do if there is a lion in your bed?**

A: Go to a hotel for the night!

Q: **What has a horn but does not honk?**

A: A rhinoceros.

Q: **Why are frogs so happy?**

A: They just eat whatever bugs them!

Q: **What happened when they invented the broom?**

A: It was an idea that swept the nation!

Knock knock.
  Who's there?
Moe.
  Moe who?
Moe knock-knock jokes, please!

Knock knock.
  Who's there?
Lego.
  Lego who?
Lego of the doorknob so I can come in!

Knock knock.
  Who's there?
Stu.
  Stu who?
It's Stu late to ask any questions!

  Q: What has a face and two hands, but no arms or legs?

  A: A clock!

Q: **What do you get when you cross a porcupine with a snail?**

A: A slowpoke.

Q: **Where does a cow go when it's hungry?**

A: To the calf-eteria.

Q: **Why did the duck set his alarm for so early in the morning?**

A: He liked to get up at the quack of dawn!

Knock knock.
  Who's there?
Minnow.
  Minnow who?
Let minnow when you plan on letting me in!

Knock knock.
  Who's there?
Gwen.
  Gwen who?
**Gwen do you think you can
  come out and play?**

Knock knock.
  Who's there?
Sherwood.
  Sherwood who?
Sherwood enjoy coming in and seeing you!

**Q: Why was the duck happy after his
  doctor's appointment?**

A: Because he got a clean bill of health.

Samantha: Who stole the poor baby octopus?

Henry: I don't know, who?

Samantha: The squid-nappers!

Q: What kind of bear doesn't have any teeth?

A: A gummy bear.

Q: What do you call a pumpkin that watches over you?

A: A body-gourd.

Q: What do you get when you cross a rabbit and a frog?

A: A bunny ribbit.

Patient: Doctor, I think I'm a chicken.

Doctor: How long have you been feeling this way?

Patient: Ever since I was a little egg.

Q: What do you call a dinosaur who's scared all the time?

A: A nervous rex.

Q: How do you know if your printer likes music?

A: When it's always jamming.

Knock knock.
Who's there?
Kanga.
Kanga who?
No, kangaroo.

Knock knock.
Who's there?
Rupert.
Rupert who?
**Rupert your left foot in, Rupert
your left foot out.**

Knock knock.
Who's there?
Henrietta.
Henrietta who?
Henrietta bug and now he has a stomachache.

**Q: Why was the caterpillar running for its
life?**

A: Because it was being chased by a
dog-erpillar!

Q: What is smarter than a talking cat?

A: A spelling bee.

Andrew: Do you know how to spell "hard water" using only three letters?

Dave: I'm pretty sure that's impossible!

Andrew: No, it isn't. I-C-E is hard water!

Q: What kind of seafood tastes great with peanut butter?

A: Jellyfish.

Q: Why is talking to cows a waste of time?

A: Whatever you say goes in one ear and out the udder.

Q: What is a whale's favorite candy?

A: Blubber gum.

Q: What do you get when you throw
   noodles in a Jacuzzi?

A: Spa-ghetti.

Q: What does a black belt eat for lunch?

A: Kung food!

Knock knock.
   Who's there?
Annie.
   Annie who?
**Annie chance I could tell you
   another knock-knock joke?**

Knock knock.
   Who's there?
Hans.
   Hans who?
Hans up—you're under arrest!

Knock knock.
  Who's there?
Jamaica.
  Jamaica who?
Jamaica good sandwich? I'm hungry!

Q: Where do bees come from?

A: Sting-apore and Bee-livia.

Tim: My dog keeps chasing people on a bike!

Tom: Why don't you put him on a leash?

Tim: No, I think I'll just take his bike away.

Q: What is as big as an elephant but weighs zero pounds?

A: An elephant's shadow.

Q: Why did the clock go back four seconds?

A: It was really hungry!

Knock knock.
Who's there?
Peas.
Peas who?
Peas tell me some more knock-knock jokes.

Knock knock.
Who's there?
Betty.
Betty who?
I Betty doesn't know who this is!

Knock knock.
  Who's there?
Wanda.
  Wanda who?
I Wanda where I put my car keys.

Q: What did the father buffalo say to his son as he left for school?

A: "Bi-Son!"

Q: Why do basketball players need so many napkins?

A: They're always dribbling!

Q: Why don't dalmatians like to take baths?

A: They don't like to be spotless.

Q: What do woodpeckers eat for breakfast?

A: Oak-meal.

Knock knock.
Who's there?
Dozen.
Dozen who?
Dozen anyone ever open their door anymore?

Knock knock.
Who's there?
Muffin.
Muffin who?
Muffin much going on around here.

Knock knock.
Who's there?
Chew.
Chew who?
I want to hang out with chew so let me in!

Q: What kind of house does a pig live in?
A: A hog cabin.

Q: Why did the cat get detention at school?
A: Because he was a cheetah.

Q: What do you call it when one cow is spying on another cow?
A: A steak out.

Q: **Why did the house go to the doctor?**

A: It had a lot of window panes.

Q: **Why did the king go to the dentist?**

A: Because he wanted a crown on his tooth!

Q: **What kind of homework do you do on the couch?**

A: Multipli-cushion.

Q: **What do you get when you cross a snowman and a lion?**

A: Frost-bite.

Q: **How do crabs call each other?**

A: They use their shell phones.

Knock knock.
  Who's there?
Window.
  Window who?
**Window I get to hear some more
  knock-knock jokes?**

Knock knock.
  Who's there?
Wade.
  Wade who?
**Wade a minute—I want to tell you
  another knock-knock joke!**

Knock knock.
  Who's there?
Sofa.
  Sofa who?
**Sofa these have been good
  knock-knock jokes.**

Q: How are As just like flowers?

A: Bees follow them.

Q: What do you get if you mix a rabbit and a snake?

A: A jump rope.

Q: Why did the bathtub need a vacation?

A: Because it was drained.

Q: Why are snails one of the strongest creatures in the world?

A: They can carry their house on their back.

Knock knock.
  Who's there?
Dwight.
  Dwight who?
Dwight key will get the door open.

Knock knock.
  Who's there?
Wheel.
  Wheel who?
Wheel you let me tell you another knock-knock joke?

Knock knock.
  Who's there?
Max.
  Max who?
Max no difference to me.

Q: What does a grizzly do on a hard day?

A: He'll just grin and bear it.

John: I'm really bright.

Jane: How bright are you?

John: I'm so bright, my mother calls me sun.

Q: How did the police know the invisible man was lying?

A: They could see right through him.

Q: What kind of animal always contradicts itself?

A: A hippo-crite.

Knock knock.
   Who's there?
Hummus.
   Hummus who?
Let me in and I'll hummus a tune.

Knock knock.
   Who's there?
Pasture.
   Pasture who?
**It's way pasture bedtime, so
   you'd better go to sleep!**

Knock knock.
   Who's there?
Conrad.
   Conrad who?
**Conrad-ulations! That was a
   great knock-knock joke!**

Q: How do you grow a blackbird?

A: Plant some birdseed.

Q: What happens when you get a thousand bunnies to line up and jump backward?

A: You have a receding hare line!

Q: Why did the robin go to the library?

A: It was looking for bookworms.

Q: What do you get when you combine a kitty and a fish?

A: A purr-anha!

Q: Why was the carpenter mad that he hit the nail with his hammer?

A: Because it was his fingernail!

Q: Why don't lobsters share their toys?

A: Because they're shellfish (selfish)!

Q: Where do shrimp go if they need money?

A: The prawn shop.

Q: What do you get when you cross an elephant with a fish?

A: Swimming trunks.

Knock knock.
  Who's there?
Abbott.
  Abbott who?
Abbott time you asked!

Knock knock.
Who's there?
Michael.
Michael who?
I Michael you on the phone if you don't answer the door!

Knock knock.
Who's there?
Ada.
Ada who?
Ada lot of sweets and now I feel sick!

Q: **What did the mother possum say to her son?**

A: "Quit hanging around all day and do something!"

Q: Why did the chickens get in trouble at school?

A: They were using fowl language.

Patient: Hey doc, I think I broke my leg in two places. What should I do?

Doctor: Don't go to those two places anymore!

Q: What do you get when you brush your teeth with dish soap?

A: Bubble gums.

Q: Why did the orange have to stop and take a nap?

A: It ran out of juice.

Q: **What do frogs like with their cheeseburgers?**

A: French flies and a croak.

Q: **What animal can jump higher than a house?**

A: All of them—houses can't jump!

Q: **What do you get if a cow is in an earthquake?**

A: A milkshake.

Knock knock.
  Who's there?
Butter.
  Butter who?
Butter open up—it looks like rain out here!

Knock knock.
Who's there?
Freeze.
Freeze who?
**Freeze a jolly good fellow, freeze
a jolly good fellow.**

Knock knock.
Who's there?
Ice cream soda.
Ice cream soda who?
Ice cream soda people can hear me!

Q: Why are fish so bad at basketball?
A: They don't like getting close to the net.

Q: What is the world's hungriest animal?
A: A turkey—it just gobble, gobble, gobbles!

Q: Why did the chef have to stop cooking?

A: He ran out of thyme.

Q: What do you get when you cross an owl and bubble gum?

A: A bird that will chews wisely.

Knock knock.
Who's there?
Francis.
Francis who?
Francis in Europe, and Brazil is in South America.

Knock knock.
Who's there?
Avery.
Avery who?
Avery nice person is knocking on the door. You should come take a look.

Knock knock.
  Who's there?
Jewel.
  Jewel who?
Jewel have to let me in soon.

Q: **What kind of photographs do dentists take?**
A: Tooth pics.

Q: **When is it bad luck to see a black cat?**
A: When you're a mouse!

Josh: **Should I go see the prairie dogs in Texas?**
Anna: Sure, Josh, gopher it!

Q: What kind of bull doesn't have horns?

A: A bullfrog.

Knock knock.
  Who's there?
Gladys.
  Gladys who?
I'm Gladys time for another
  knock-knock joke.

Knock knock.
  Who's there?
Yule.
  Yule who?
Yule never know who it is unless
  you open the door!

Knock knock.
  Who's there?
Stan.
  Stan who?
Stan back, I'm coming in!

Q: What do cobras put on their bathroom floor?

A: Rep-tiles.

Q: What do you do if your dog steals your spelling homework?

A: Take the words right out of his mouth.

Q: What do computer programmers eat when they're hungry?

A: Bytes of chips.

Q: Why did the policeman go to the baseball game?

A: He heard someone had stolen second base.

Knock knock.
Who's there?
Sadie.
Sadie who?
If I Sadie magic word, will you let me in . . . P-L-E-A-S-E?

Knock knock.
Who's there?
Ivan.
Ivan who?
Ivan idea—let's tell more knock-knock jokes!

Knock knock.
  Who's there?
Les.
  Les who?
Open the door and Les be friends!

Q: **What do you call a cow with two legs?**

A: Lean beef.

Q: **What do you get when you throw a pony in the ocean?**

A: A seahorse!

Q: **What does a goat use when it's camping?**

A: A sheeping bag.

Q: Where do you learn to cut wood?
A: At boarding school.

Knock knock.
  Who's there?
Mustache.
  Mustache who?
I mustache you a question, so let me in!

Knock knock.
  Who's there?
Norway.
  Norway who?
**There is Norway I'm going to just
  stand here, so open the door!**

Knock knock.
Who's there?
Water.
Water who?
Water you doing later?

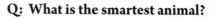

Q: What is the smartest animal?

A: A snake, because no one can pull its leg.

Q: What has four wheels and flies?

A: A garbage truck!

Q: What do you get when you combine an elephant and a skunk?

A: A smell-ephant.

Jimmy: **Did you hear about the kid who got hit in the head with a can of pop?**

Bobby: No, is he okay?

Jimmy: **Yep, he's just lucky it was a soft drink.**

Q: Why do seagulls fly over the sea?

A: If they flew over the bay they'd be bagels!

Q: What kind of tree has the most bark?

A: The dogwood tree.

Q: What has two heads, four eyes, six legs, and a tail?

A: A cowboy on a horse.

Q: What do you give a mouse on its birthday?

A: Cheese-cake.

Knock knock.
  Who's there?
Radio.
  Radio who?
Radio not, here I come!

Knock knock.
  Who's there?
Snow.
  Snow who?
Snow use—I'll never run out of knock-knock jokes!

Knock knock.
  Who's there?
Jess.
  Jess who?
Jess me and my shadow.

Q: What do skunks like to eat when they're hungry?

A: Peanut butter and smelly sandwiches.

Q: When is a noodle a fake?

A: When it's an im-pasta.

Q: What kind of dog is good at chemistry?

A: A Lab-rador retriever.

Q: What are the funniest fish at the aquarium?

A: The clown fish.

Q: Who helped the mermaid go to the ball?

A: Her fairy cod-mother.

Q: What do you call a pig that is no fun to be around?

A: A boar.

Q: Why did the elf get in trouble with his teacher?

A: He didn't do his gnome-work.

Q: What do you get when you cross a dinosaur and gunpowder?

A: Dino-mite.

Knock knock.
  Who's there?
Iguana.
  Iguana who?
Iguana come in, so please open up!

Knock knock.
  Who's there?
Marilee.
  Marilee who?
Marilee, Marilee, Marilee, Marilee, life is but a dream!

Knock knock.
  Who's there?
Hammond.
  Hammond who?
**Let's make some Hammond
  eggs for breakfast.**

**Q: What do you call a polar bear in
    Hawaii?**

A: Lost!

**Q: How do you know when it's been
    raining cats and dogs?**

A: When you step in a poodle.

Q: Why can't you trust a pig?

A: It will always squeal on you.

Q: **What is a skeleton's favorite instrument?**

A: A trombone.

Q: **Why was a pig on the airplane?**

A: Because its owner wanted to see pigs fly.

Suzy: **I'm so smart I can sing the whole alphabet song!**

Jimmy: That's nothing. I can sing it in lower case and capitals!

Q: **Which creatures on Noah's ark didn't come in pairs?**

A: The worms—they came in apples.

Q: **What do you get when you cross a
dentist and a boat?**

A: A tooth ferry.

Knock knock.
  Who's there?
Waddle.
  Waddle who?
**Waddle you do if I tell another
  knock-knock joke?**

Knock knock.
  Who's there?
Manny.
  Manny who?
**How Manny knock-knock jokes
  do you want to hear?**

Q: **What is a drummer's favorite vegetable?**
A: A beet.

Q: **Why did the lobster get grounded by his parents?**

A: He was always getting himself in hot water!

Q: **What do you get when you play tug-of-war with a pig?**

A: Pulled pork.

Q: **Why did the snake lose his case in court?**

A: He didn't have a leg to stand on.

Q: **Why do birds fly south for the winter?**

A: Because it's too far to walk, and their feet won't reach the pedals on a bicycle!

Q: What does a monster put on top of his hot fudge sundae?

A: Whipped scream.

Q: Did you hear about the new restaurant they put on Mars?

A: I hear the food is out of this world.

Q: How do you know when a rhino is ready to charge?

A: It gets out its credit card.

Knock knock.
   Who's there?
Ear.
   Ear who?
Ear is another knock-knock joke—are you ready?

Knock knock.
   Who's there?
Lionel.
   Lionel who?
**Lionel always get you in trouble,
   so tell the truth!**

Knock knock.
   Who's there?
Mushroom.
   Mushroom who?
**There's mushroom for improvement
   on that last joke.**

Q: **What happened to the bee after he had
   four cups of coffee?**

A: He got a buzz.

Q: **What happens when strawberries are sad?**

A: They become blueberries!

Q: **Why was the bird nervous after lunch?**

A: He had butterflies in his stomach.

Joe: **Can you believe that I ate six helpings of spaghetti last night?**

Bill: Well, I wouldn't put it pasta!

Q: **Why did the suspenders have to go to jail?**

A: They held up a pair of pants.

Q: **What do you get when you cross a monkey and a peach?**

A: You get an ape-ricot.

Q: **Why did the book join the police force?**

A: It wanted to go undercover!

Q: **What do you call a story about a giraffe?**

A: A tall tale.

Knock knock.
  Who's there?
Rhino.
  Rhino who?
Rhino you want to let me in.

Knock knock.
  Who's there?
Anita.
  Anita who?
Anita hear another knock-knock joke!

Knock knock.
  Who's there?
Roach.
  Roach who?
I roach you a letter but I wanted to deliver it in person.

Q: **Why was the crow on the phone?**

A: Because he was making a long-distance phone caw!

Q: **Why did the plant go to the dentist?**

A: It needed a root canal!

Q: Why are chickens so bad at baseball?

A: Because they're always hitting fowl balls.

Patient: **Doctor, I have a problem. I think I'm a moth.**

Doctor: I don't think you should be seeing me. I think you need a psychiatrist!

Patient: **I know, but I was on my way there and I saw you had your light on.**

Q: How does Moses make his tea?

A: Hebrews it.

Q: Why couldn't the fish go shopping?

A: It didn't have anemone.

Q: Why did the reporter go to the ice-cream parlor?

A: He wanted to get the scoop!

Q: What kind of dogs can tell time?

A: Watchdogs.

Knock knock.
Who's there?
Zany.
Zany who?
Zany body want to come out and play?

Knock knock.
Who's there?
Barbie.
Barbie who?
Barbie-Q.

Knock knock.
  Who's there?
Waddle.
  Waddle who?
**Waddle you give me if I stop
  knocking and go away?**

Q: **What did the orange say when it was
  stepped on?**

A: You hurt my peelings!

Q: **Why are snails shy at parties?**

A: They don't want to come out of their shell.

Q: **How did the gorilla fix its bike?**

A: With a monkey wrench.

Q: How do fish pay their bills?

A: With sand dollars.

Knock knock.
Who's there?
Cash.
Cash who?
No thanks, I'd rather have some peanuts.

Knock knock.
Who's there?
Nicole.
Nicole who?
I'll give you a Nicole if you let me in.

Knock knock.
  Who's there?
Toby.
  Toby who?
Toby or not Toby; that is the question,
   and you'll have to open up to find out!

Sally: **What is a mummy's favorite**
      kind of music?

 Bill: I'm not sure.

Sally: **Wrap music!**

Q: What do you call bears with no ears?

A: B!

Q: How does a pig get to the hospital?

A: In a ham-bulance.

Q: What do you get when you cross a snake with dessert?

A: A pie-thon.

Knock knock.
Who's there?
Ken.
Ken who?
Ken I tell you another knock-knock joke?

Knock knock.
Who's there?
Ash.
Ash who?
It sounds like you're catching a cold.

Knock knock.
 Who's there?
Boil.
 Boil who?
Boil you like this next joke!

Q: **Why can't you ever trust an atom?**

A: They make up everything!

Dave: **What do you get when you cross an airplane, a car, and a cat?**

 Bill: I give up.

Dave: **A flying car-pet!**

Q: **What is something that has to be broken before you can use it?**

A: An egg!

Q: When does a hot dog get on your nerves?

A: When it's being a brat—it's the wurst.

Q: A cowboy arrives at the ranch on a Sunday, stays three days, and leaves on Friday. How is that possible?

A: His horse's name is Friday.

Q: Why did the boy always carry his piggy bank outside?

A: In case there was change in the weather.

Margie: Would you like to go camping this weekend?

Minnie: No, that sounds too in-tents for me.

Q: Why did the rabbit need to relax?

A: He was feeling jumpy.

Knock knock.
Who's there?
Arthur.
Arthur who?
Arthur any more funny knock-knock jokes?

Knock knock.
Who's there?
Theodore.
Theodore who?
Theodore is locked so please let me in!

Knock knock.
Who's there?
You.
You who?
You-hoo, it's me, can I come in?

Q: What kind of homework do you do in a taxi?

A: Vocabulary.

Q: Where do fish like to sleep?

A: On their water beds.

Q: Why did the whale cross the ocean?

A: To get to the other tide.

Q: How can you learn more about spiders?

A: Check out their web-site.

Q: Where can you learn to make ice-cream treats?

A: In sundae school.

Q: Why can't you trust what a baby chick says?

A: Talk is cheep.

Q: What do you do if a cow won't give milk?

A: You mooove on to the udder one.

Q: What do you call a deer with no eyes?

A: No eye deer (no idea).

Knock knock.
  Who's there?
Eddy.
  Eddy who?
Eddy-body home?

Knock knock.
  Who's there?
Diane.
  Diane who?
I'm Diane to see you, so open the door!

Knock knock.
  Who's there?
Megan.
  Megan who?
**It's Megan me mad that you
  won't open the door!**

Q: What did the dog say when he rubbed
  sandpaper on his tail?

A: "Ruff, ruff!"

Q: What do you get when an elephant
  sneezes?

A: You get out of the way!

Q: What do fish like to sing during the holidays?

A: Christmas corals.

Q: What has a head and a tail, but no body?

A: A penny.

Knock knock.
Who's there?
Mickey.
Mickey who?
**Mickey won't fit in the keyhole,
can you let me in?**

Knock knock.
Who's there?
Jimmy.
Jimmy who?
If you Jimmy a key, I'll let myself in.

Knock knock.
  Who's there?
Luke.
  Luke who?
**Luke through the window and
  you'll see who's knocking.**

Q: Why was the library so busy?

A: It was overbooked.

**Q: What is the difference between a fish
  and a piano?**

A: You can't tuna fish (tune a fish).

Q: Why did the skunk cross the road?

A: To get to the odor side!

Q: **What kind of fish comes out at night?**

A: A starfish.

Q: **Why was the bird wearing a wig?**

A: Because it was a bald eagle.

Q: **What did the almond say to the psychiatrist?**

A: "Everybody says I'm nuts!"

Q: **Why do penguins carry fish in their beaks?**

A: They don't have any pockets.

Q: **Where do trout keep their money?**

A: In a river bank.

Knock knock.
Who's there?
Donut.
Donut who?
Donut make you laugh when people tell knock-knock jokes?

Knock knock.
Who's there?
Bruce.
Bruce who?
I'll Bruce my knuckles if I keep on knocking!

Knock knock.
Who's there?
Canoe.
Canoe who?
Canoe come out and play?

Q: How do you keep a restaurant safe from criminals?

A: Use a burger alarm.

Q: What do you get from a pampered cow?

A: Spoiled milk.

Q: What do you call kids who play outside in the snow?

A: Chilled-ren.

Q: Why was the snake so funny?

A: His jokes were hiss-terical.

Knock knock.
Who's there?
Sarah.
Sarah who?
Sarah reason you're not opening the door?

Knock knock.
Who's there?
Amanda.
Amanda who?
Amanda fix the plumbing is here.

Knock knock.
Who's there?
Leaf.
Leaf who?
Leaf me alone so I can read my joke book!

Q: Why did the burglar steal the eggs?

A: He likes his eggs poached!

Q: Who helps pigs fall in love?

A: Cu-pig.

Q: What does a cat eat for breakfast?

A: Mice Krispies.

Q: Why did the baker go to work every day?

A: He really kneaded the dough!

Knock knock.
  Who's there?
Howl.
  Howl who?
Howl I open the door if it's locked?

Knock knock.
  Who's there?
Everest.
  Everest who?
Everest, or is it work, work, work?

Knock knock.
  Who's there?
Billy Bob Joe Penny.
  Billy Bob Joe Penny who?
**Seriously, how many Billy Bob
  Joe Pennys do you know?**

Q: **What kind of automobile is the same
  going backward and forward?**

A: Racecar.

Q: **Why did the elephant quit his job?**

A: He was working for peanuts.

Q: What kinds of keys are easy to swallow?
A: Cookies.

Josh: Do you think change is hard?
Joe: I sure do—have you ever tried to
bend a quarter?

Knock knock.
Who's there?
Spell.
Spell who?
W-H-O.

Knock knock.
Who's there?
Thatcher.
Thatcher who?
**Thatcher was a good knock-knock
joke. Can you tell another one?**

Knock knock.
Who's there?
Juicy.
Juicy who?
Juicy any monsters under my bed?

Q: What do you call your dog when it goes deaf?

A: It doesn't matter—it can't hear you anyway!

Q: Why did the boat go to the mall?

A: It was looking for a sail.

Q: What do you call a lazy kangaroo?

A: A pouch potato.

Q: What do you get when you cross a fish and a tree branch?

A: A fish stick.

Knock knock.
Who's there?
Moo.
Moo who?
Make up your mind—are you a cow or an owl?

Knock knock.
Who's there?
Wendy.
Wendy who?
Wendy wind blows de cradle will rock.

Knock knock.
  Who's there?
Wanda.
  Wanda who?
Wanda come out and play?

Q: What is a reptile's favorite movie?

A: The Lizard of Oz.

Q: What do you call a boy with no money in his pocket?

A: Nickel-less.

Q: What do you call someone with no body and no nose?

A: No-body knows.

Q: **What is the best time to see the dentist?**

A: At tooth-thirty.

Q: **What sound do porcupines make when they kiss?**

A: Ouch!

Q: **Where do you take a hornet when it's sick?**

A: To the wasp-ital.

Q: **What do you find at the end of everything?**

A: The letter "g."

Q: Why couldn't the polar bear get along with the penguin?

A: They were polar opposites.

Knock knock.
   Who's there?
Auto.
   Auto who?
You really auto tell me some knock-knock jokes!

Knock knock.
   Who's there?
Alpaca.
   Alpaca who?
Alpaca suitcase for our vacation.

Knock knock.
Who's there?
Ringo.
Ringo who?
Ringo round the rosie!

Q: What kind of dog cries the most?

A: A Chi-wah-wah.

Q: How did the marching band keep their teeth clean?

A: With a tuba toothpaste.

Q: What do you call a bunny's prized possessions?

A: Hare-looms.

Q: What do you feed a teddy bear?

A: Stuffing!

Knock knock.
  Who's there?
Dewy.
  Dewy who?
**Dewy have a key to open this door or do
  I have to go through the window?**

Knock knock.
  Who's there?
Otter.
  Otter who?
You otter open the door and let me in!

Knock knock.
Who's there?
Alex.
Alex who?
Alex-plain when you open the door!

Q: How do you make friends with everyone at school?

A: Become the princi-pal.

Q: What did the picture say when the police showed up?

A: "I didn't do it—I've been framed!"

Q: What kind of buttons does everyone wear?

A: Belly buttons.

Sally: Can you believe I gave my pigs a bath?

Susie: That's a bunch of hog wash!

Knock knock.
Who's there?
Alma.
Alma who?
Alma knock-knock jokes are really funny!

Knock knock.
Who's there?
Who.
Who who?
What, are you an owl or something?

Knock knock.
 Who's there?
Zoo.
 Zoo who?
Zoo think you can come out and play?

Q: What do you get when you cross a cow and a rabbit?

A: You get hare in your milk.

Q: What do dogs have that no other animals have?

A: Puppies.

Q: Why do fish make good lawyers?

A: Because they like de-bait.

Q: When can an elephant sit under an umbrella and not get wet?

A: When it's not raining.

Q: What sometimes runs but never walks?

A: Your nose!

Q: What kind of dogs chop down trees?

A: Lumber Jack Russells.

Q: Why do rhinos have so many wrinkles?

A: Because they're so hard to iron.

Q: How do you keep a dog from barking in the back seat of the car?

A: Put him in the front seat of the car.

Knock knock.
   Who's there?
France.
   France who?
France stick closer than a brother.

Knock knock.
   Who's there?
Abby.
   Abby who?
Abby stung me on the leg—ouch!

Knock knock.
   Who's there?
Fannie.
   Fannie who?
**If Fannie body calls, tell them
   I went to the store.**

Q: How many months have 28 days?

A: All 12 of them do!

Q: Why can't you tell a joke to an egg?

A: It might crack up!

Q: Why was the bee's hair all sticky?

A: It used a honeycomb.

Q: Why are sheep so gullible?

A: It's easy to pull the wool over their eyes.

Q: What do you get when a pig does karate?

A: Pork chops!

Emma: Can February March?

Leah: No, but April May.

Q: Why was the skeleton laughing?

A: Somebody tickled its funny bone.

Q: How does a farmer count his cattle?

A: With a cow-culator.

Q: How does a mother hen know when her chicks are ready to hatch?

A: She uses an egg timer.

Knock knock.
  Who's there?
Queen.
  Queen who?
Queen as a whistle!

Knock knock.
  Who's there?
Nobel.
  Nobel who?
There was Nobel so I had to knock!

Knock knock.
  Who's there?
Ima.
  Ima who?
Ima really glad to see you today!

Q: **What do you get when a rhinoceros goes running through your garden?**

A: Squash.

Q: **How do you have a party on Mars?**

A: You have to planet.

Q: **What was the elephant doing on the freeway?**

A: I don't know—about 10 miles per hour?

Q: **What do you give a pig that has a cold?**

A: Trough syrup!

Q: Why were the lamb and goat such good friends?

A: Because they had a very close relation-sheep.

Q: What do you call a fish with no eyes?

A: Fsh!

Q: What did the C note say to the D note?

A: "Stop! You're under a rest."

Q: How do you know which end of a worm is the head?

A: Tickle the middle and see which end laughs.

Knock knock.
Who's there?
Butcher.
Butcher who?
Butcher hand over your heart when you say the Pledge of Allegiance.

Knock knock.
Who's there?
Doris.
Doris who?
If the Doris locked I can't come in.

Q: Which has more courage, a rock or a tree?

A: A rock—it's boulder!

Q: How did everyone know that the lion swallowed the bear?

A: His stomach was growling.

Q: What game do leopards always lose?

A: Hide and seek—they always get spotted.

Q: What did the firefly have for lunch?

A: A light meal.

Q: What do you get when you cross a penguin and a jalapeño?

A: A chilly pepper.

Q: Which word in the dictionary is always spelled wrong?

A: WRONG, of course!

Q: What did the mother lion say to her cubs before dinner?

A: "Shall we prey?"

Q: **How do you keep a skunk from smelling?**

A: Hold its nose!

Knock knock.
Who's there?
Misty.
Misty who?
I misty chance to see you—will you let me come in?

Knock knock.
Who's there?
Landon.
Landon who?
Is it true cats always Landon their feet?

Knock knock.
  Who's there?
Tank.
  Tank who?
You're welcome!

Q: **What do a mouse and a wheel have in common?**

A: They both squeak.

Q: **Why did the apples want to hang out with the banana?**

A: Because it was so appeeling.

Q: **What do you call an insect that complains all the time?**

A: A grumble-bee.

Q: **What kind of birds like to stick together?**

A: Vel-crows.

Knock knock.
   Who's there?
Shelby.
   Shelby who?
Shelby comin' around the mountain when she comes!

Knock knock.
   Who's there?
Kent.
   Kent who?
I Kent see why you won't just open the door.

Knock knock.
  Who's there?
Dishes.
  Dishes who?
Dishes me, open up!

Q: **What did the tornado say to the race car?**

A: "Can I take you for a spin?"

Q: **What do you get when you cross a dog and broccoli?**

A: Collie-flower.

Q: **Why did the pony get sent to his room without supper?**

A: He wouldn't stop horsing around.

Q: What language do pigs speak?

A: French, because they go "Oui, oui, oui" all the way home!

Q: Why did the cat go to the beauty salon?

A: It needed a pet-icure.

Q: What does a moose like to play at parties?

A: Moose-ical chairs.

Q: What is a lightning bug's favorite game?

A: Hide and glow seek.

Q: Why do dragons sleep all day?

A: Because they like to hunt knights.

Knock knock.
Who's there?
Lena.
Lena who?
**Lena little closer and I'll tell
you another joke.**

Knock knock.
Who's there?
Handsome.
Handsome who?
Handsome food to me, I'm hungry!

Knock knock.
Who's there?
Meg.
Meg who?
**Meg up your mind—are you going
to let me in, or aren't you?**

Q: What do you call a cow that can't give milk?

A: A milk dud.

Q: Did you hear about the dog that didn't have any teeth?

A: Its bark was worse than its bite.

Q: What's brown and sticky?

A: A stick.

Q: What do you get when a barn full of cows won't give milk?

A: Udder chaos.

Knock knock.
  Who's there?
Isaac.
  Isaac who?
Isaac of knocking so please let me in!

Knock knock.
  Who's there?
Colin.
  Colin who?
From now on I'm Colin you on the phone!

Knock knock.
  Who's there?
Elsie.
  Elsie who?
Elsie you later!

Rob Elliott is the author of several popular joke books for kids, including *Laugh-Out-Loud Jokes for Kids*, which is a *USA Today* and *Wall Street Journal* bestseller. It is also one of Amazon's Top 20 Bestselling Children's Books of All Time. Rob's joke books have sold more than 2.5 million copies. He lives in West Michigan, where in his spare time he enjoys laughing out loud with his wife and five children. Learn more at www.laughoutloud jokesforkids.com.